How Hard Could It Be?

Scott Phillips

To Gene + Anne
Thanks for all your
encouragement!

Scott Ph——

Phil 4:13

ISBN: 1468142399
ISBN-13: 978-1468142396

DEDICATION

To my wife Mary and our children, Greg, Abby, and Trent.
I am blessed beyond words to have you in my life.

To my parents, grandparents, and great-grandparents for
leaving a Godly legacy to follow.

CONTENTS

ACKNOWLEDGMENTS

Writing and publishing a book is never a "one-man show." I do not have the words to adequately thank my wife Mary for all the encouragement and support she has given me throughout our marriage and specifically during this project. I'd like to thank Audrey Brubaker for the fine job of editing the drafts and gently pointing out my many grammatical mistakes. Much gratitude also goes to Dr. Bruce McCracken, Founder of House on the Rock Ministries, for his guidance over the past few years and for giving me the opportunity to "find my voice" as a speaker and writer. Finally, I wish to thank my colleague and friend Jeff Kime for his countless hours of help as we walked through the publishing process and for his constant encouragement. It is truly a privilege to be a part of the House on the Rock Family Ministries team.

FOREWARD

I first met Scott Phillips when he was a student in my "Marriage and Family Ministry" class at Lancaster Bible College. I could tell even back then that God had instilled in him a deep passion for helping families, and when he inquired about an internship at House on the Rock a few years later I didn't hesitate to bring him on board. Since that time I have personally witnessed Scott's growth not only as speaker and writer, but as a husband, father, and follower of Jesus Christ.

At House on the Rock we strive to encourage men, equip parents, and enrich marriages, and I believe that Scott has accomplished all three of those goals with this book. We often speak to couples about the "oneness" quality of marriage that God desires for us, and for many couples one of the main obstacles to achieving that oneness is a lack of understanding of the unique trials and triumphs of each other's "worlds." Because Scott has spent a considerable amount of time both at home and in the workforce he is exceptionally qualified to speak to those challenges.

Writing in his usual humor-filled manner, Scott raises some tough issues that all couples need to discuss and work through in *How Hard Could It Be?*, and I believe that couples (and small groups) will find the questions and prayer topics at the end of each chapter to be particularly helpful in getting those discussions going! As an avid reader (and a man!), I also appreciate Scott's easy-to-read style of writing and am thrilled that this is a book that I know men can and will enjoy.

Our ministry gets its name from a parable Jesus tells during His "Sermon on the Mount" in Matthew 7:24-29. While the foolish man built his house on the sand, the wise man built his house on the "rock," that is, on Jesus himself and on God's Word. As we often say in our workshops, it is not a matter of if the "storms of life" will come, it is only a matter of when. It is my hope that this book will help you in building your relationship with your spouse and in building a strong home that has its foundation built "on the rock."

I'm excited for the positive impact that this book will have on so many marriages and families, and as you read it I want you to know that we will be praying for you and your spouse.

Bruce McCracken, Ph.D.
President and Founder, House on Rock Family Ministries

Chapter One

Introduction

"For I know the plans I have for you," declares the Lord, "plans to prosper you and not to harm you, plans to give you hope and a future." – Jeremiah 29:11

The 1987 hit film *The Untouchables* portrays a fictionalized account of government agent Eliot Ness's pursuit, arrest, and conviction of famous mobster Al Capone. Included in the movie is a famous scene where Capone sends his men to "eliminate" a member of Ness's "Untouchables" team, a veteran police officer named Jimmy Malone (played by Sean Connery). The audience watches as the Capone gangster slowly stalks a seemingly unaware Malone in his apartment. As the hoodlum pulls a large knife out of his coat, Malone turns around while holding a shotgun, revealing that he knew what was happening all along. The camera shifts back to the gangster, whose facial expression is a mix of fear, wonderment, and confusion. Malone then delivers one of the movie's signature lines (slightly edited), "Isn't that just like a [fool]? Brings a knife to a gun fight."

The saying "bringing a knife to a gun fight" had been around well before *The Untouchables*, but the movie helped to bring it into popular American lingo. It basically means to be woefully unprepared for a challenge or to be or feel vastly inadequate. In my case, "bringing a knife to a gun fight" is a great metaphor for the period of time that I spent as a stay-at-home dad. All through this book I hope to share some of the lessons that being at home with my kids has taught me, as well as to illustrate my hapless efforts to apply them. Looking back, I'm still not sure how I survived, except for the grace of God and the help of my wonderful wife, Mary.

The Beginning

But first, a little background is probably in order. After graduating from college and a short stint as a high school teacher, I was hired as the Director of Human Resources at a local food manufacturer and distributor. In that role I was responsible for the care and well-being of the 130+ workforce during three shifts. I hired, I promoted, I counseled, I disciplined, and at times, I fired. As a member of upper management, I had a lot of responsibility and had to make many difficult decisions. My cell phone was always on so that I could attend to whatever issue arose throughout the week (and sometimes the weekend).

During this time we had two children at home, our son Greg (who was 5) and our daughter Abby (who was 2), and Mary was teaching math very part-time at a local college. Life was everything I thought it should be – we lived in a nice neighborhood, we were active at our local church, and we were comfortable with our roles (I was the primary provider; Mary took care of the kids and home). I had every reason to be happy, yet there was something (or rather Someone) tugging at my heart. Was this really the pinnacle? Or did God have another plan in mind for me?

I had been wrestling with God for awhile over the direction of my life. A planner by nature, I never took step one without knowing what steps two, three, and four were going to be. My plans always included God – I was raised in a Christian home and cannot remember a time when I did not believe that Jesus died for my sins. I credit my 4th and 5th grade Sunday school teacher for leading me through the "sinner's prayer." Then, in 2003, Mary and I suffered a miscarriage with our second pregnancy. It was a life changing experience for me. For the first time I realized I was not totally in control of my life. Until that point, things had gone pretty much according to plan. I began to question whether or not I had truly trusted my life to God and whether I was really pursuing God. Finally, sometime during the summer of 2006 I broke down and told God that I was ready to let Him be in charge.

That's when I realized the truth of Jeremiah 29:11 – "For I know the plans I have for you,' declares the LORD, 'plans to prosper you and not to harm you, plans to give you hope and a future.'" But not only did God have plans for me; He also had a sense of humor! Not long after that moment of surrender, Mary came home with news that would change everything. Her college wanted her to come to work on a full-time basis. What did I think?

The Decision

Practical person that I am, I suggested that Mary at least find out what they were offering. Due diligence and all that. A couple of days later she came home with a report. It was an "offer we couldn't refuse." Suddenly our safe, comfortable little world was being shaken like a snow globe. We both felt that Mary should pursue the college's offer, but we weren't excited about putting two small children into daycare full-time.

Now, don't misunderstand me. I realize that many families require both parents to work as a financial necessity. Even though it meant watching our dollars, Mary and I were fortunate enough to be able to have one parent at home. Of course, if she was working, there was only one other person available to watch the kids!

Shortly thereafter I had the painful conversation with my boss informing him that I would be resigning from my position to stay at home with our kids. As tempting as having dual incomes was, Mary and I wanted one of us at home. My boss took the news well, although I received a bit of good-natured (at least, I think it was good-natured!) teasing about the transition. I quickly became known as "Mr. Mom" after the country song by the group Lonestar that had hit #1 in late 2004 and was still popular at the time. "Mr. Mom" tells the first-person story of a stay-at-home dad and how his expectations of a life of easy living were quickly shattered by the challenges of raising his kids. The song begins with these lyrics:

Lost my job, came home mad
Got a hug and kiss and that's too bad
She said I can go to work until you find another job
I thought I like the sound of that
Watch TV and take long naps
Go from a hard working dad to being Mr. Mom

The Aftermath

I have to admit that when I walked through the door on December 30, 2005, and left the company for good, I was pretty sure that was how it was going to go for me as well. Of course, I never said this publicly! Just like the dad in the song, I quickly realized my folly. I had gone from being in charge of the care, well-being, and discipline of 130 or so adults to being in charge of the care, well-being, and discipline of two small children. Guess which one was harder! It wasn't long until "Mr. Mom" became the theme song for my life, particularly the chorus:

> *Pampers melt in a Maytag dryer*
> *Crayons go up one drawer higher*
> *Rewind Barney for the fifteenth time*
> *Breakfast, six naps at nine*
> *There's bubble gum in the baby's hair*
> *Sweet potatoes in my lazy chair*
> *Been crazy all day long and it's only Monday Mr. Mom*

As a stay-at-home dad I've had my share of triumphs and successes and my share of mistakes and failures. Many times I wanted to pull my hair out, and occasionally I cried out to God, "Really? This is what turning over my life to you looks like?" Yet through it all He helped me to persevere and taught me so much about the joys and privilege of being a dad.

Throughout these following chapters I've tried to encapsulate as much about what God taught me during my time as a stay-at-home dad as I can in seven general principles. While nothing is new under the sun, perhaps my experiences will frame them in a new way that can both encourage and challenge you. My hope is that couples will read this book together and then discuss the questions at the end of each chapter. The chapters are short, so guys, you can do this!

As you do that I would encourage the "working" spouse (whether it's the husband or the wife) to seek to understand more fully the challenges that face the spouse who stays at home. I firmly believe that your relationship will be better because of it!

Chapter Two

"What Does She Do All Day?"

"Now we ask you, brothers and sisters, to acknowledge those who work hard among you, who care for you in the Lord and admonish you." - 1 Thessalonians 5:12

Seeking Satisfaction

Before I became a stay-at-home dad, I would often be out the door by 6:30 in the morning. My days consisted of phone calls, meetings, computer work, more meetings, interviews, and some more meetings. I usually arrived at home around 5:00 in the afternoon. It didn't happen often, but sometimes the house looked exactly the same when I arrived as when I had left in the morning. Perhaps toys would still be lying around, the laundry not put away, or the dishes not done. Now I am not that foolish of a man, so I would never say this aloud, but I have to confess to thinking, "What does she do all day?"

It wasn't long after I started staying at home that I learned the answer! I had no idea the amount of work it takes to run a home. I had envisioned doing a few chores in the morning, maybe taking the kids to a park, having lunch, and then putting the kids down for naps and "me" time. I think I may have had that "normal" day twice in the four years that I stayed home!

I had realized going in to this change that work would need to be done every day. After all, I had observed Mary doing it for many years. But I was missing one key aspect to this work – the two little people who were constantly "undoing" all that hard work. Toys were picked up only to be strewn across the floor minutes later. The laundry was a never-ending chore. No sooner had I washed the last dirty shirt than three more would appear in the hampers. At one point I started keeping track of the outfits that our daughter went through each day (an average of 5, with a high of 10. I believe she set some sort of indoor/outdoor record that day). Swept floors were filthy by the next meal, and I firmly believe that dirty sippy cups somehow breed in the kitchen sink.

On top of all of that, each day brought a new errand to run: Monday was a trip to the bank; Tuesday was reserved for grocery shopping and story time at the local library; Wednesday was another trip to a different library, and so on. Things only got worse when Greg started kindergarten, as he needed picked up each day at 11:45 am sharp. I soon learned that the "stay-at-home" part of my new job description was pretty laughable!

By nature I am a planner and a list maker. I take great satisfaction in setting goals for each day and working hard to get them completed. At the office that was possible on many days. At home that was impossible on most days. Why? Because I had a little boy and a little girl (and later, a second little boy named Trent) who also had things that they wanted done each day! And their "task list" rarely matched mine. I learned that part of my "job" at home included the things on their lists, like reading books together, building garages and race tracks out of blocks, playing in the backyard, and practicing bike riding in the driveway. We even had an occasional (don't tell anyone) tea party, complete with costumes!

Many days getting "my" list completed would have meant ignoring my kids. I'll be honest; some days that happened. *The funny thing was, I didn't get that "satisfaction" that I was hoping for on those days.* The house may have been cleaned and the laundry done, but my attention-starved kids weren't happy, and they often would overwhelm Mary with requests for attention when she got home. I became an afterthought, and who could blame them? I hadn't been there for them throughout the day because I had "my" list that needed accomplished, so as soon as someone was there to show them love, they forgot all about me.

I'm not sure if Paul had any experience as a stay-at-home dad or not, but Ephesians 6:4 surely sounds as if he did! *"Fathers, do not exasperate your children; instead, bring them up in the training and instruction of the Lord."* That verse has new meaning for me. There are certainly many ways that we dads (and moms) can exasperate our kids, but I doubt there is a more efficient one than ignoring them and their needs! We are called to teach and train our kids in the way of the Lord, and nowhere in the scriptures does it say that teaching and training should only occur after all the chores are done.

In fact, Deuteronomy 6:6-7 makes it clear what God wants our first priority as parents to be— *"These commandments that I give you today are to be upon your hearts. Impress them on your children. Talk about them when you sit at home and when you walk along the road, when you lie down and when you get up."* In other words, God is saying, "Hey parents, your job isn't to make sure your kids get to a Sunday school class once a week. I want you to be continually investing in them and showing them how to walk in my ways. That's job #1."

11

Not coincidentally, some of my most satisfying days at home were ones where a little work got done and a lot of attention was given. Everyone was happy on those days. The kids were content; Mary didn't get overwhelmed the moment she walked in the door; and I got a few things checked off the list. But you know who the key person was to making those good days great? The family member who had been at work all day – Mary! Why? Never once did she ask me why the house wasn't picked up, or the laundry folded, or a full-course homemade meal on the table when she came home. Those of you who work – you have no idea how "freeing" that is. Sure, Mary always made sure to note if the house was picked up, but she never expected it. Since she had been the one who had stayed at home first, she already knew what I was finding out – some days everything won't get done, and that's okay.

Working Hard or Hardly Working?

On one of the last days at the company, a coworker came up to me to say goodbye. Part of our conversation included this exchange:

> Him – "So you are really doing this, huh? Staying home with the kids?"
>
> Me – "It's going to be different, that's for sure."

Him – "Man, I think that is great. Wish there was some way to convince my wife to go to work. I'd love to be the one who gets to stay home and do nothing all day. It would be nice to not be the one that has to get up and go to work each day!"

Me – "Well, I don't think that's how it's going to work, exactly."

Him – "Well, she doesn't just sit around of course. But it's not like working here. I'm tired when I get home!"

To be fair, the guy was actually trying to encourage me (I think), but his attitude revealed a lot about what he thought of his wife's role in their partnership. Sadly, I'm pretty sure he is in the majority when it comes to this attitude. And there certainly were days when my perspective was a bit skewed.

One particularly frustrating day late in my career at the company, I came home in a complaining frame of mind.

Me – "I'm exhausted. I must have sat through five meetings today and I had a couple of interviews. In between that I was on the phone all afternoon. How was your day?"

Mary – "Well Abby was up three times overnight, so we are all running low on energy. Both kids are now sick and throwing up, so I have been dealing with that all day. I managed to get the grocery shopping done in between cleaning up puke so we'd have something for dinner, but then a friend from church called wanting to stop by so I ran around the house picking it up. I'm just now getting the laundry done and dinner is running late. Sorry about your meetings."

Me – (Humbled silence)

I thought I "worked" hard at the office, but that kind of work paled in comparison to what needed done at home. I found myself just as tired (if not more) at the end of the day. One of the things that men can do that drives their wives absolutely nuts is to act as if we know what it is like to walk in their shoes. Guys, trust me on this – we don't. It is important that we understand (and communicate that we understand) how valuable the work of our wives is to us and to our family. And if our wife is a working mom, balancing job responsibilities, home responsibilities, child-care and everything else, then we REALLY don't have a clue!

Many of us are familiar with Ephesians 5:25 – "Husbands, love your wives, just as Christ loved the church and gave himself up for her…" This passage is read at many weddings and is frequently the basis for sermons on marriage. Less familiar to us, however, is 1 Peter 3:7 – "Husbands, in the same way **be considerate** as you live with your wives and **treat them with respect**…"(emphasis mine). So we are reminded that we men are not only to love our wives, but also to be considerate and treat them (and their role in the family) with respect.

I have to admit that many times I failed to respect the work that Mary did in managing our home, and while I have a new-found respect for that role in the family, I can still fail at being considerate of her. One of the most powerful ways that a husband can do that is to show his wife that he appreciates her and is deeply grateful for all that she does each day. How can husbands do that? Here are a few suggestions:

- Ask her how her day was BEFORE talking about your day. Ask if she has had any downtime, and if not, make sure she gets some.
- Take the kids for a walk, bike ride, playground trip, etc.
- Do the dishes and clear the dining table.
- Give her a chance to go out for lunch or dinner with a couple of friends.

- Plan a date night. Take care of ALL of the details
 (babysitting, reservations, etc.).

Of course, one of the best ways to show that we appreciate the jobs that our wives do is to actually do it ourselves occasionally! Encourage your wife to get away for an overnight or a weekend and then run the home as she does. No cheating by sending the kids to Grandma's house or ordering out for each meal! One more thing – for some reason men think that there is a verse in the Bible that gives them a free pass on going to worship on a Sunday morning if their wife is away. There isn't. I know because I checked...twice!

The comedian Jeff Foxworthy once said, "Whatever cleaning goes on on the planet, women do 99% of it. But see, women are not as proud of their 99% as men are of our one! We clean something up, we're gonna talk about it all year long. It might be on the news, you don't know." What makes the joke funny is that it isn't that far from the truth!

Being at home with small children is hard work. It requires long hours. It requires tons of patience. It requires the ability to read "Billy and Bobby Visit the Firehouse" 10 straight times without wishing that Big Red the Fire Truck would run over Firedog Spot. It is an honorable profession, one that God clearly approves of.

Discussion Questions

1. What describes a "satisfying" day for you? What happens that leaves you with that deep sense of satisfaction and accomplishment? What might you need to change in order to have more of those days? What can your spouse do to support you in those changes?

2. What about your job (whether you work at home or at a workplace) do you wish your spouse understood better? What does your spouse have a good understanding of?

3. How can each of you be more considerate of the stresses of each other's work? How can you work together to give each other the "down time" that you both need?

Prayer Topic

Spend a few moments praying together. Thank God for the work that your spouse does and the contribution that your spouse makes to the family. Ask Him to help you to be able to show your appreciation for your spouse's work every day.

Chapter 3

So, What Do You Do?

"Honor her for all that her hands have done, and let her works bring her praise at the city gate." – Proverbs 31:31

Once I became a stay-at-home dad, I began to dread meeting other men for the first time. In our American culture when two men meet, the first question they ask of each other after being introduced is "So, what do you do?" Sometimes we do it just because we are making small talk, but more often than not it is our way of sizing up the other guy. After all, status can be instantly achieved by telling other people our occupation. Of course, the higher the wages and greater the perceived responsibility an occupation has, the more status the man has.

With this "system" firmly in place, I had no shot. I tried to avoid the question as best as I could, but sooner or later I had to "confess" to staying at home and taking care of our kids. The reaction was almost always the same – the other guy would have the same look on his face as if I had just declared that I was a cult leader, then say "Ohhhhh….Okay" and start to end the conversation as quickly as possible and begin to look for another guy to measure himself against. Clearly, he had me beat. I might as well have worn a sign that said, "Don't Bother – Does Nothing All Day." Even after I went back to school to pursue a Master's degree, I still came up short.

Frankly, the women that I met at activities like Story Time at the library weren't much better. Most assumed I worked 2nd or 3rd shift. Others thought I was in-between jobs. A few just assumed I was a deadbeat. They wouldn't say that, of course. They would just make sure their kids didn't sit anywhere near mine. Some marveled at my wife, saying that they couldn't imagine having to work all day and then come home to make dinner (for the record – neither could Mary, since I cooked). One of our relatives wondered if we had hot dogs every night (for the record – No).

The conversation with a bewildered mom that sticks in my mind the most went something along these lines:

> Confused Mom – "So do you work at night, or do
> you just have flexible hours that you can be at
> school during the day?"

> Me – "Neither, actually. I'm staying at home to take
> care of the kids. My wife teaches at a local
> college."

> Confused Mom, apparently thinking that I had just
> lied to her face – "Are you serious?"

> Me – "Yep, it's unusual but it's working for us."

At this point you would have thought that she would have dropped the conversation and backed slowly away from me like so many others. Not this lady!

> Confused Mom – "I've seen you at all of these
> school functions and just had to ask.
> Sometimes I've seen your wife here, but
> mostly it's been you. You looked like
> someone, you know, respectable, but I just
> had to ask."

To this day I have no idea what the point of that statement was, but I think she was trying to compliment me on the fact that I didn't look like an unkempt hillbilly. Somehow, the conversation got worse:

Me – "Well, I am going to school while I am at home, so there are times she pinch hits for me."

Confused Mom – "So she cooks and cleans in the evening when she gets home?"

Notice how she assumed that I was incapable of doing either of these tasks!

Me – "No, I take care of all that. I'm fairly good at it."

Confused Mom – "Well, I'm sure she helps a lot. Good luck, you'll need it."

Me – "Oh, I'm already lucky. I don't have to talk to you anymore."

Just kidding, I made up that last statement. The rest of it is practically verbatim. I wish I could say that this conversation was an exception, but I had plenty that were similar to it.

No Respect

"I get no respect, NO RESPECT I tell ya!" The late comedian Rodney Dangerfield often punctuated his jokes with that line, which has become something of a "catch-phrase" in our culture. Stay-at-home parents could certainly identify with him! Regardless of whether the one working at home is the mom or the dad, the world simply does not see the work that is done around the home as having equal value to the work that is done at the office or job site.

As an aside…

Please don't misunderstand me. I'm not making a judgment on families where both parents work. For some it is a financial necessity; for others it is a personal choice. Either way, I don't believe that scripture specifically prohibits it. What I do believe that scripture makes clear is that work at home is to be valued and made a priority for the family. 1 Timothy 5:8 tells us that believers need to provide for their families. For many years (decades, centuries) the person best able to do that was the husband, since he had the highest earning potential. That is not necessarily the case today.

In both Titus 2:3-5 and 1 Timothy 5:14, Paul speaks about the wife being the one who manages the home. After my experience being the one at home, I certainly see the wisdom in that! Mary is more gifted than I am when it comes to managing the home. In neither case, however, does Paul *mandate* that the wife work solely at home. In Titus he calls on older women to *encourage* younger women in

22

their duties at home, and in Timothy he *counsels* women to manage the home. Indeed, in many families it is the best thing for the family for Mom to stay home.

Paul's teaching must be balanced with what is taught in Proverbs 31, where we are given the famous (or infamous, depending on your view) "Wife of Noble Character." While the woman is described as working hard at home, she also buys property and earns money with it (verse 16) and makes linen garments to sell them (verse 24). The Bible commentator Dr. Thomas L. Constable provides good advice for any couple regarding these verses:

> "However, husband and wife should agree that this is best for the family. She should make sure her motives and priorities are in order before committing herself to such a job. Is the income essential to meet needs or wants? Is she doing the work to avoid her other higher priority responsibilities? Is she hoping that her job or career rather than her relationship with God and her family members will satisfy her needs?"

Those are great questions for couples to talk about as they decide what is best for their family and how they can make the home a priority. Contrary to what the secular world would have us believe, there is a great freedom that comes with walking with God! Because of that freedom that Mary and I decided to have me stay at home for a while, and because of that freedom, I returned to the workforce after a few years (more on that in the concluding chapter).

We don't even have any positive terms to accurately describe the work of those who stay at home. "Stay-at-home mom" (or dad) implies that is all that happens, when in fact, many stay-at-home moms and dads rarely spend all day at home. "Homemaker" is a little better since it at least implies that some work takes place, but it is really just the government's term for the role since the name is gender-neutral (it's been used since the 1970s, when gender-specific language was deemed discriminatory). The most unfortunate term, in my opinion, is the traditional "housewife," which often conjures up images of those famous "moms" from 1950s television (i.e. June Cleaver) but has recently reentered the pop culture with two television series – the fictional *Desperate Housewives* and the reality show *Real Housewives of…,* neither of which portray the stay-at-home parent in any kind of positive light. Truly, stay-at-home parents get "no respect" from modern society.

It's Up to Us

With secular society increasingly apathetic or even hostile to the stay-at-home parent, the desire to "band

together" with other like-minded couples is very strong.
Churches have begun to recognize this, and many
communities have at least one weekday morning Bible study
or "MOPS" (Mothers of PreSchoolers) groups.
Unfortunately for me, there weren't many options for men.
I often thought I should start a "POPS" group (Papas of
PreSchoolers)!

While these kinds of groups are great for providing
fellowship and encouragement to the stay-at-home parent
and for fostering an atmosphere of mutual respect, they
cannot replace the sense of respect of one's work that the
stay-at-home spouse needs from his or her working partner.
It wasn't until I was the one staying at home that I truly
understood that.

As always, the Bible is our guide in this endeavor. In
describing the Wife of Noble Character in Proverbs 31:31,
the writer says, "Give her the reward she has *earned,* and let
her works bring her praise *at the city gate"* (emphasis mine).
Note the two ways that respect can be shown to the stay-at-
home spouse. First, they should be allowed to enjoy the
fruits of their labor because they have earned it. God does
not call for those who take care of the home to drudgingly
work all the time. Second, they are to be praised publicly for
their work. Now I ask you, who is in the best position to be

able to fulfill this need in their life? The answer, of course, is their working spouse!

Working spouses can show respect to their stay-at-home partner by making sure he or she gets a break from time to time to relax and enjoy life. It communicates that we understand that the work is hard and that it is valued. We should also find cause to publicly praise our spouse for the work that they do. We should be telling others what a great job they do managing the house, working it into our casual conversations. And we should be doing this praising with our spouse present! As I mentioned before, there were several times soon after our transition that we would be visiting with some friends when the wife would comment how she couldn't possibly manage both the home and a job. Of course, the statement was made as a way of encouraging Mary, but it also implied that I wasn't doing anything to help. I do not have the words to adequately express how it felt when Mary would reply, "Actually Scott does a great job at home; he takes care of almost everything."

Why is showing respect for your spouse's work so important? Well, first of all it is obeying God. Romans 13:7 says that we are to "Give to everyone what you owe them: If you owe taxes, pay taxes; if revenue, then revenue; if respect, then respect; if honor, then honor." Second, it is obviously going to help our marriage relationship. Romans 12:10 says that we are to "Be devoted to one another in love. Honor one another above yourself." This command is important in all of our relationships, but especially in our marriage.

The Bible also tells us that showing respect to our spouse yields great benefits for our own spiritual walk. Showing respect to our spouse helps our prayer life (1 Peter 3:7), enables us to serve in leadership roles (1 Timothy 3:4-5), and allows God's peace to be with us (Philippians 4:8-9).

Just as important, mutual respect between spouses provides a model for their children to follow. Many of us are familiar with the command to honor our father and mother, first given in Exodus 20:12 and repeated multiple times through the scriptures. We often quote this commandment in the context of children obeying their parents (that is proper – Paul actually used the word obey in Ephesians 6:1), but this idea of honor goes much further than that. We are to respect our parents as the ones who gave us life and as God's representatives to us here on earth. This learned behavior and character trait can then be extended to the other relationships in our kids' lives and, eventually, to their future spouse.

But how do children learn to show respect and honor? *By watching Mom and Dad.* When our sons see me showing Mary respect and honor for her role in the family, her status as a child of God, and as a woman, they begin to understand how a Godly man and husband should act and (hopefully) begin to show this attitude toward others in general and to women in particular. Likewise, when our daughter Abby sees how Dad treats Mom, she will learn to recognize when this attitude isn't present in a man and (again, hopefully) steer clear of him in spending meaningful time together.

Once a working spouse begins to have a better understanding of the nature and difficulty of the work that is needed to manage the home (which we discussed in Chapter 1), and begins to understand the lack of respect that the stay-at-home parent receives from the world (we discussed in Chapter 2), a true home/work partnership can happen. The marital bond will be stronger, and the home will be more secure and peaceful.

Now, what does a working spouse need to better understand about the challenges of parenting those kids whom we stay home with? We'll tackle those ideas in the next few chapters.

Discussion Questions

1. What can your spouse do to clearly communicate the respect that he or she has for your role in the family?

2. Why do you think that the stay-at-home parent has lost so much "status" in the world? What has happened to help cause this drop?

3. How can each of you model respect and honor for your children? What do they need to see and hear in the home?

Prayer Topic

Spend a few moments praying together. Give thanks for the tremendous freedom that God gives you in choosing what is best for your family. Ask Him for guidance, opportunity, and encouragement to implement some of the strategies that you have discussed. Pray for your children and ask that God would give you wisdom in raising up men and women who are respectful of the opposite sex.

Chapter 4

It's 8 AM and I Want to Give Up

"Indeed, there is no one on earth who is righteous, no one who does what is right and never sins." –
Ecclesiastes 7:20

"What is going on here?" Greg and Abby had been arguing back and forth for some time, and my patience was running thin. As I stomped downstairs to put my little fighters on the dreaded "time-out," I could feel my blood pressure rising. It hadn't been a good morning up to that point. We had all gotten up late and had to rush Mary out the door. I hadn't had coffee yet, and I couldn't find my car keys, which meant we weren't going to get all the errands done that I thought needed done. Everyone was grouchy, and no one was cooperative.

"I've had enough! You kids have worked against me all morning. I can't stand it anymore!" And with that they both burst into tears. Not exactly a "Father of the Year" moment. Read that first paragraph again. What were the issues? It wasn't the kids' fault that we had gotten up late and had to rush around. They weren't the ones who made the coffee. They weren't the reason why I couldn't find the keys (I am notorious for misplacing them). They didn't set the errand agenda for the day. In fact, they had very little to do with my frustration, but I was taking it out on them. I had failed them.

The Myth of the Perfect Parent

Although in our "head" we know that we aren't expected to be perfect parents, in our "heart" we feel as if we should be. After all, our homes are Christ-centered! What a tremendous advantage our families should have in comparison to non-believing families. So why doesn't it work out that way?

Where do these feelings come from? Perhaps it is a misapplication of scripture. In Matthew 5:48 Jesus concludes His famous "Sermon on the Mount" with this instruction: "Be perfect, therefore, as your heavenly Father is perfect." Talk about setting the bar high! It's a wonder that the crowds kept following him after that. If perfection is to be our goal, then how is it possible to not get discouraged and ready to give up?

Some have attempted to answer this question by translating the text in a manner so that the word used for "perfect" in Greek is "mature." I can see why that works for some. I've been around plenty of "mature" people who've lost their temper or made mistakes. The problem is that while the Greek *teleios* can be used to mean mature (as it does in Ephesians 4:13, for example), it is not used that way in Matthew 5. Why? Because we know from the totality of scripture that God is perfect! So saying that we should be "mature" as our heavenly Father is "perfect" just doesn't make sense. Clearly, Jesus meant perfection in the sense of being without fault or blemish.

So how, then, are we to respond to this instruction, particularly in the world of parenting? We must first avoid viewing perfection as an outward-only quality. Parents have a tendency to feel that if we mess up and are therefore blemished as parents, then we are forever tainted. That is how the Pharisees viewed it. While God is concerned with our actions, He is more concerned with our inner self: purity of our thoughts, attitudes, and desires. Perfection is simply a goal that we have on this side of eternity, and it should be pursued earnestly. We should desire to be a better parent today than yesterday, for example. We should take steps to avoid repeating mistakes.

But while we are called to pursue perfection, we are not to be fixated by it. Although our mistakes as parents should concern us, we should not become paralyzed by them. Too often parents shy away from taking any parenting action for fear of taking the wrong action. We do not serve and worship a God who is ready to "smite" us at the first chance He gets. I believe that He understands all too well the challenges of dealing with disobedient children (after all, He deals with me on a daily basis), and is ready to forgive us for our mistakes and help us learn from them. So if God allows us to be less than perfect, we should allow ourselves that same freedom as well. The pursuit of perfection is not the ultimate way of living for the believer; the pursuit of knowing and loving God is.

Our homes are going to be filled with sin, hurt, tension, and all those other bad things that we hope to avoid. The goal of a Christian parent is not to raise our kids and manage our homes in such a "perfect" way so that those qualities never exist. That's impossible, if for no other reason than we are all selfish, depraved people living in a fallen world that is desperately in need of a Savior.

The difference for the Christian home, if we are on our journey towards perfection, is for it to be filled with grace, forgiveness, understanding, patience, and love; for they are the "perfect" qualities of our Father. As parents, we should be concerned with whatever mistakes we make and whatever hurt is happening in our homes, but we should be more concerned with how we respond to those situations. Our attitudes toward our spouses and children and to our neighbors are the means through which we can begin to achieve the qualities of perfection that Jesus is referring to in Matthew 5.

One humbling way that I have learned to fill my home with those "perfect" qualities of God is to be willing to apologize to my kids when I mess up. This isn't easy, because they aren't always the most gracious givers of forgiveness! For example:

> Me – "Greg, I'm sorry for snapping at you this morning. I was frustrated, but that isn't a good reason to yell. Can you forgive me?"

> Greg –"Don't worry about it, Dad. Someday you'll get it together."

> Me – "Uh, thanks."

> Greg – "I figured you'd be grouchy this morning since the Redskins lost last night."

Me – "Why don't you find something to play now?"

I have to admit that the comfort of knowing that I don't need to be a perfect parent was and is much easier to feel when I am working outside of the home. I think that it is important for working spouses to understand the enormous amount of pressure (and guilt) that stay-at-home parents put on themselves to make sure that their kids "turn out right."

The Myth of the "Normal" Child And the Guilt It Causes

Success in the workplace is a fairly easy thing to measure. Our companies give us goals (sales figures, customer service ratings, department profitability levels, etc…) and we work to meet them. At least once a year we get a formal review where our boss tells us whether or not we are doing well, and hopefully we get a raise as a reward for our hard work. String together enough good reviews and we get promoted to a higher paying job, or at least one with more responsibility. People usually have no problem identifying a successful business person.

For the stay-at-home parent, however, success is much harder to define. Our "success" is tied directly to how well our kids are doing, because they are to be our main responsibility. So when our kids struggle in school, socially, or developmentally, we stay-at-homers can feel like failures, even when we are doing a great job. I didn't understand that when I was the working spouse, but I understand that now.

In an attempt to provide some objective measures of whether or not a child is progressing "normally," we as a society have developed all sorts of benchmarks that our kids should reach at certain ages. There are benchmarks for when they should be walking and when they should be talking, for example. There are benchmarks for how tall they should be and how heavy they should be and even how large their head should be. I understand the value in them; they help us know what areas our kids may need extra help in. But the standards seem to be increasingly harder to reach. My children needed to know their ABC's and how to count to 20 and a whole host of other things before they even started kindergarten. I went to kindergarten to learn those things!

Add to this pressure for our kids to measure up the myriad magazine articles, books, educational toys, and other products designed to "help" parents raise their kids better. While all these resources can be helpful, they often communicate a message to parents that they aren't doing things as well as they can and should be. And parents hear that message loud and clear! We begin to constantly search out the latest popular parenting guide and we join support groups so that we can measure how we are doing beside other parents in our area (I know that isn't the stated goal of those groups, but if we are honest that is what happens). We watch video series and TV shows devoted to being better parents, all in the hope that if we can somehow be the best, most perfect parent possible, our kids will turn out okay.

And what happens when our children aren't just like everyone else? Guilt descends on us like a heavy blanket. Johnny not hitting the 50th percentile? It's because of something we did wrong. Susie doesn't walk yet? It's our fault. Timmy isn't the highest achiever in preschool? Obviously we've failed him. It's hard for Sally to make friends? There must have been something we should have done differently. We should have read to our children more, or hugged them more, or taken more time for them, and so on.

For the longest time when Abby was young she was below the charts in height and weight (Greg barely made them). The doctor was very concerned that we weren't feeding her enough and what we were feeding her was too low in calories. Despite the fact that Abby looked like a perfectly healthy preschooler and that based on her parents' height she probably was never going to be real tall, we immediately changed her diet and tried to get her onto those charts. Guilt started creeping into our lives because of it, and we had to consciously choose to not let it get to us. Despite all of our efforts, she rarely made it onto the charts. Of course, today she is a beautiful little girl who, while petite, is well within the "normal" range for her age!

The guilt continues to pile up, and soon each time we lose our temper or miss a school function or feel as if we've let our kids down in any way, we hear this voice inside our head saying, "I'm the worst parent in the world....I can't do this....my kids are going to flounder and IT'S ALL MY FAULT!" Because we see it as our responsibility that our kids succeed in every area of life (after all, that's why we stay home), we absorb any of their "failures" as our failures. The working spouse, whose perceived primary responsibility for the family is to provide, usually does not share in the burden (or at least shares only a small part of it). As long as the family is provided for, that spouse is doing his/her job!

In a "Guilt-Off," Moms Always Win

I learned many things during my time as a stay-at-homer, but one concept that has clearly been demonstrated to me time after time is that moms feel guiltier when their kids fail than dads do, regardless of who is working and who is at home. If a child is struggling and Mom is at home, then she feels guilt because she was home and not parenting well enough. On the other hand, if a child is struggling and Mom works outside of the home, then she feels guilt because she wasn't home to parent more. Either way, she struggles with guilt.

Men just aren't wired that way. It's not that we don't feel guilt if our kids are struggling, but we usually aren't consumed by it. While I did feel like a failure at times when I was home with the kids, more often I felt guilt when money was tight, because I was responsible for the family being provided for, even if I was primarily at home. Ask any dad if he would feel guiltier if his kids were failing or if the family was struggling financially, and he will choose the lack of money almost every time.

There Is Hope

You can quickly see how unhealthy this kind of thinking is. To avoid getting sucked into a "shame spiral," I believe that couples need to talk about two key areas of parenting:

1.   Defining (or, more likely, redefining) what "success" in the home looks like for them. Don't be trapped in by whatever standards the world wants you to have. Search the scriptures for God's standards.

2. Determining the signs that one (or both) parents are starting to feel an unhealthy amount of guilt. Guilt can cause all sorts of relational issues within a family. When we see our spouse beginning to show signs of being burdened by guilt, how will we help them overcome it?

Noted author Olive Wyon once said, "For many people the heavy responsibilities of home and family and earning a living absorb all of their time and strength." Many of us parents feel the weight of those words every day. There is hope, however, because God does not expect us to be perfect in our parenting. In fact, a family that is imperfect yet continues to display grace, forgiveness, and love to each other is one of the most powerful examples of God's faithfulness that exists! As Wyon says, "Yet such a home – where love is – may be a light shining in a dark place, a silent witness to the reality and the love of God." Amen!

Discussion Questions

1.   How can we avoid being fixated on perfection as a parent? What can the working spouse do to help the stay-at-home spouse with this task?

2.   What are some of the warning signs of being burdened by guilt that you see in your spouse? What about yourself? What can you do to help each other avoid a "shame spiral"?

3.   Do you agree that moms feel guiltier than dads when the children are struggling in an area of life? Why or Why Not?

Prayer Topic

Spend a few moments praying together. Ask God to help you avoid judging yourself by the false standards of the word. Ask Him for relief from guilt that burdens you. Pray for your family and ask Him to help you be a light to the world around you as you address whatever challenges you face as a family.

Chapter 5

The Big Yellow Fellow Is Not the Enemy

"So then, each of us will give an account of ourselves to God." – Romans 14:12

I still remember that first day of school for Greg. The sleepless night before. The long, slow walk to the bus stop. The slouched shoulders and worried look. Wiping away tears. The hug as the bus pulled up, lasting just a little longer than normal. And that was me! Greg was fine. He ran to the bus stop, jumped up and down as the bus pulled up and gave a big smile and wave as he bounded up the bus steps. Meanwhile, I was barely keeping it together.

Fairly typical stuff for your oldest child's first day of school! But here's the real interesting part – it happened again the next year for first grade, and every year since. And please don't ask me how I handled it when my little girl went to school for the first time. Now, I'm not an overly emotional guy, but something about that first day of school really gets to me. If fact, I'm getting a lump in my throat just writing this!

The Loss of Exclusive Influence

A good friend once pointed out to me that as a stay-at-home parent, I had virtually exclusive influence on my kids. I could control who they played with, what music they listened to, and what TV shows they watched. Even if I couldn't be physically with them at any given moment, I could control who was. As I watched that yellow school bus pull away and tearfully watched Greg bravely wave to me one last time out the window, it dawned on me that this time of life was over for him and for me. The sense of loss that I felt was very real, and (despite being warned that this would happen) as I watched my exclusive influence disappear down the road, I was truly in mourning.

It wasn't until Greg and Abby starting going to school that I realized just how limited my power as a parent is. They listened to songs on the bus that I wouldn't have played on our radio. They learned about TV shows and movies that we didn't watch in our house. They learned some new words. Slowly, I could see the "world" influencing them. My "job" as a parent was getting harder.

God understands the difficulty of parenting. He knows all too well the corrupting influence that the elements of this fallen world can have on our kids. So He wants us to be as involved and influential in their lives as possible. Proverbs 22:6 implores, "Train a child in the way he should go, and when he is old he will not turn from it." This proverb should be all the motivation we parents need to invest all we have into our kids. After all, a vibrant walk with the Lord is what we all want for our kids, right?

If we believe (and I do) that the Bible is the inspired and inerrant Word, then verses like Proverbs 22:6 can be troubling, especially when it appears that our children are turning from the way they should go. But those verses needn't be troubling to us. When we read and interpret the Bible we need to understand what type of literature we are reading. Proverbs may be best described as "wise sayings that are generally true." They are not guarantees.

Unfortunately (as mentioned in the previous chapter) some parents feel tremendous guilt when they see their children stray from the faith, feeling as if they have somehow failed. The fact is that our faith as parents can't save our kids. As they grow it is up to them to choose to walk with God.

Romans 14:12 says, "So then, each of us will give an account of himself to God." God understands that our influence has limits. He created each of us with the ability to turn from truth. So we shouldn't be blaming ourselves when our kids choose wrongly.

Working spouses should understand that they need to be constantly encouraging and reminding their partner that they are doing their best and that they are parenting as a team. One of the worst responses to a child's poor choices is for parents to start judging or blaming one another's efforts.

Unfortunately, the local church is often a place of judgment for parents of kids who have strayed from the path. Even well-meaning comments like, "You are such good parents; I just can't imagine what you could have done differently," can often sound like judging to hurting parents. They hear the person implying that the parents should have done something differently; they just can't think of what that should have been.

Bad News and Good News

For parents, the "bad news" is that we will steadily lose influence with our kids as they grow older. Their friends and peers will continually become larger influences on what clothes they wear, what TV shows and movies they watch, what activities they choose, and especially what moral decisions they make. Children who once depended on us for every need in life will suddenly seem to have no need for us at all!

While this transition is hurtful for all parents, I believe that it affects the stay-at-home parents even more. After all, they have been the ones to provide for the majority of those needs over the years. Many times the stay-at-home parents' main sense of self-worth is derived from the fact that their children need them. Once that need is gone, the parent can really struggle with knowing what to do next.

Here's the truth about this time of transition – it's supposed to work this way! We really don't want our kids to be dependent on us for the rest of their lives. In fact, we've truly succeeded as parents when they are able to live on their own successfully! When each of our kids' wedding day arrives sometime down the road, I really don't want to be sitting there thinking "I'm not done with him/her yet! There's still some stuff I want to teach them!"

In the days of America's westward expansion, it was common for families to travel together as part of wagon trains. At night they often circled the wagons as protection from the elements and to keep the animals safe from predators. Parents will sometimes do something similar with their kids. They will limit their kids' access to anything that isn't overtly "Christian," keeping them close to home (or the church) at all times.

Now, I am not suggesting that we shouldn't encourage our kids to participate in church activities or shouldn't try to steer them towards Christian friends. Clearly, we want as many positive influences around them as possible! That's a big part of our job, and we certainly have to consider the element of protection in determining what we allow our kids to participate in.

But while I do believe that it is our job as parents to protect our kids, it's also important that we don't always "circle the wagons" around our kids whenever danger is lurking. They need to gain experience in dealing with all that the world throws at them. They need to face temptations. They need to deal with rejection. They need to stand up to immorality. Let's face it; those things are going to happen to them sooner or later, either as children, teens, or adults. I believe that it is far better for it to happen while they are still under our guidance and care. Even if (or rather, when) they fail, at least they will do so while we as parents are still in a place where we can help them pick up the pieces and help them work through their mistakes.

There is "good news" when it comes to influencing our kids as well. While we will lose our exclusive influence, we always have the most influence. As powerful as the world's influence can be, it cannot overtake parental influence. Now, to be fair, when our kids are in their late teens this ratio is fairly even, but even then we as parents still have the majority. In fact, once our kids reach their 20s, we even begin to regain some influence.

Mark Twain is credited with saying, "When I was a boy of fourteen, my father was so ignorant I could hardly stand to have the old man around. But when I got to be twenty-one, I was astonished by how much he'd learned in seven years." How true that statement is. While it may be hard to see our influence rapidly decline during our kids' teen years, we can take solace in knowing that it is only a temporary drop.

Discussion Questions

1.   In what ways have you seen the limits of your influence as a parent? How is the influence different when you are staying at home as opposed to working?

2.   Is your church a place where you feel supported as a parent when your children are less than perfect? How can you be more supportive of other parents in your congregation?

3.   What in the world is influencing your kids right now? How can you work together as a team to help your children face the world and not "circle the wagons" too tightly around them?

Prayer Topic

Spend a few moments praying together. Pray very specifically about the things and people who may be having a negative influence in your children's lives. Ask God to give you wisdom in knowing when to allow your kids to make mistakes and when to protect them from mistakes.

Chapter 6

The Relationship Is More Important Than the Relation

"Fathers, do not embitter your children, or they will become discouraged." – Colossians 3:21

My daughter Abby's birth was an exciting 18 hours of my life. Our first child, Greg, had arrived a week late, so as we reached the two-weeks-to-go point for Abby we figured we had plenty of time. Then Mary's water broke. Flying around the house we got everything packed and headed out the door. After dropping Greg off with Mary's parents, we headed to the hospital, me fighting the urge to drive like NASCAR legend Dale Earnhardt. I'll spare you the details from here, but let's just say that things got real interesting in a hurry and I was there every step of the way.

The next day I walked over to an elderly neighbor to share the good news of Abby's arrival. As I recounted all the happenings of the previous 24 hours, I noticed a wide grin beginning to form on his face. As I wrapped up my tale of triumph, he commented that things surely had changed since his daughter was born. When I asked him what he meant, he explained that when his wife went into labor, he dropped her off at the front of the hospital where the nurses took her in and told him to go home and wait for a call. Try doing that today, dads.

The old English proverb that "children should be seen and not heard" dates the whole way back to at least the 15th century according to some scholars. In general, it reflects an attitude that what a child thinks, feels, or wants is secondary to what an adult thinks, feels, or wants. Because of that attitude, some parents (especially dads) have kept their children at a distance relationally. This distance is most prevalent when the children are small.

When I was working, it was very easy for me to defer to my wife when it came to relating to our kids. Quite frankly, I didn't feel as if I had the patience to sit there and listen to their stories or spend an hour going through the cycle of building a tower of blocks only to have our kids knock them down. It didn't seem as if there was much of a point to it all, and I figured that once the kids grew up a little, I would "jump in" then.

Once I started staying home, I quickly realized that those times of building the same tower of blocks, or "fixing" the same toy jeep, or reading the same story, are not really about playing with our kids. Those times were really about investing in my relationship with them. Those times were about building a connection to them that will last for a lifetime.

One thing that I have learned about life (and it was reinforced during my time at home) is that our relation to someone is not nearly as important as our relationship with them. That is a wonderful truth, because we basically have no control over our relation to someone. God determined who our parents would be and who our children would be. He alone gave us our grandparents, aunts, and uncles. We inherited those relations at birth.

Our relationship with them, however, is something that is largely in our control. We can decide how much time we spend with someone, how much we share with them, how much we listen, how much we care.

One of my older neighbors mentioned that the one way he knew that his father loved him when he was growing up was the occasional time that his father would rest his hand on my neighbor's head. Our kids need more than that. It shouldn't surprise us that many kids have a deeper relationship with Mom than with Dad. Besides the obvious fact that most moms spend more time with their kids than most dads, they usually are better at relating to them.

Why? Part of the reason is related to how women are wired to be more relational than men. But another big part of it is that being relational was modeled for them by their mothers. The generational cycle continues repeatedly. And it works for (or against, depending on your perspective) dads as well. They keep their distance relationally for their kids because that is what was modeled by their dads. Many of today's dads have trouble saying "I love you" to their kids because it was never said to them.

Time, Time, Time

The phrase "quality time" entered our culture in the 1970s and has since grown in usage. It essentially means devoting all one's energy into a relationship for a short period of time. As our society has become increasingly "busier," the belief in the idea of "quality time" has become the deliverance for many parents and spouses. After all, if one is too busy for quantity time, at least one can have quality time.

As a working parent I was a firm believer in quality time, but as a stay-at-home parent I now see the value in quantity time! Simply put, quantity time yields quality time. Quality time can sometimes be scheduled, but usually it appears out of nowhere while we are spending quantity time with our families. My relationship with each of our children grew exponentially when I became a stay-at-homer, simply because I was around them more. Often quality time would come for 10 or 15 minutes several times throughout the day.

When you think about it, this makes sense. Have you ever seen your relationship with someone grow when you were constantly apart? Neither have I. Yet too many parents cling to the false hope of quality time when their children are younger, only to see their children reach the teenage and young adult years with little or no relationship to speak of.

In Galatians 6:7, Paul writes, "Do not be deceived; God cannot be mocked. A man reaps what he sows." Paul is talking specifically about the support of Christian workers, but the general principle can be used for a host of applications. If we sow seeds of apathy, indifference, or neglect into our children when they are young, we shouldn't be surprised when we harvest a relationship with our children that is cold and distant when they become adults. Likewise, we can't "sow" a row and expect to get an "acre" of harvest! If we only plant a "row" of quality time with our kids, we shouldn't expect an "acre" of harvest in the form of plenty of time together when they are adults.

Why is this so important? Why should parents be so concerned about their relationship with their kids? Hebrews 12:5-6 states:

> And you have forgotten that word of
> encouragement that addresses you as sons:
> "My son, do not make light of the Lord's
> discipline, and do not lose heart when he
> rebukes you, because the Lord disciplines
> those he loves, and he punishes everyone he
> accepts as a son."

Why can I accept discipline from my heavenly Father? Because I know that He loves me and ultimately wants the very best for me in my life. Now, I usually don't like His discipline, and sometimes I kick and scream a little bit! But I do accept it. The same is true for our children. The only way that they will accept the correction that I give them is if they know that I love them and ultimately want the best for them.

That is why the relationship is so important. If I do not cultivate a meaningful relationship with my kids, then any correction I bring into their life (as severe as discipline or as gentle as advice) will be viewed suspiciously by them. They will look for motives behind the correction other than my wanting what is best for them.

Those who have been remarried and find themselves parenting stepchildren will often find that their new sons and daughters rebel against any correction they give them. The reason for this often has nothing to do with the kids "liking" their new stepparent; it's because the new stepparent has yet to have sufficient time to prove that he or she loves the children. Younger kids will accept correction from stepparents earlier than teens, but even then it may take up to two years! That is why it is so critical for the biological parents to step in and provide correction for their kids (even if that wasn't their role in their first marriage).

The same concept applies to all families. If one parent (again, stereotypically the dad) is constantly away from the family and not connecting to the kids relationally and then tries to step in to provide correction, things will not go well. The kids do not feel loved, and therefore they can start to believe (whether it is actually true or not) that the parent has only what is best the parent in mind, not what is best for the kids.

In the area that I grew up and currently live in it is typical for a father to work 50-60 hours a week at his job and then have a variety of hobbies (hunting, golfing, riding

ATV's) that take him away from his family even more. Many of these men then wonder why they aren't connecting with their kids!

It's Been Sure Nice Talking to You

In 1974 Harry Chapin recorded his only #1 hit song, "Cats in the Cradle." Written in 1st person, the song tells the story of a father who is too busy to spend time with his son, always giving the vague promise of "I don't know when, but we'll get together then, son." The song is famous for its chorus line "The cat's in the cradle and the silver spoon, little boy blue and the man in the moon." The eerie song then "turns" at the end as the now grown boy does not have time for his father, telling him "It's sure nice talking to you Dad."

As a father, the song is almost haunting to me (Chapin himself once said that the song "scares him to death") because I can see how easily the father/child relationship can go down that path. For many of us dads (I'm speaking mainly to dads here, but all of this can apply to moms) the pull of work is strong, and if we are not careful it can pull us away from our families. We are great at rationalizing our work priority.

As working parents, we often justify our time spent at work as a necessity in order to provide for our families. The Bible is very clear in its instruction to work, but the fact remains that God intends for our priorities to be our relationship to Him, to our spouse, to our kids and then (and only then) to our work. If we place work anywhere else on our list of priorities, we aren't living according to God's plan. Again, according to God, quantity time IS quality time!

So what can the working parents do? Unfortunately, there may not be an easy answer. Perhaps cut back on hobbies for a while. Perhaps sacrifice some pay (and adjust the budget) in order to be able to work less. Perhaps put off buying the latest "toy." Perhaps clear out days on the calendar when we will not schedule anything so that we can spend those days with our families. Perhaps decide that we don't need to watch 15 hours of football every weekend in the fall and winter...or that we don't need to see all 162 Phillies games (ouch, that one hurt to type!). You get the idea. Tough decisions may be needed, but it will be worth it.

What can the stay-at-home parent do to help? Because stay-at-home spouses have "quantity time" built in to their schedules (some more than others, depending on the kids' ages and activities), their relationship with their kids is often very strong. Praise God for that, and then pray for wisdom and opportunity for your spouse to develop his or her relationship with the kids. Encourage your kids to spend as much time as possible with your working spouse. Help guard the family calendar from becoming so full of activities that the family rarely gets to just be a family!

I close this chapter with a story told by child psychologist David Elkind, recalling a conversation between his son and three other boys at his son's nursery school:

It so happened that I was sitting and observing a group of boys, including my son, who sat in a circle nearby.

Their conversation went like this: Child A: "My daddy is a doctor and he makes a lot of money and we have a swimming pool." Child B: "My daddy is a lawyer and he flies to Washington and talks to the president." Child C: "My daddy owns a company and we have our own airplane."

Then my son (with aplomb, of course): "My daddy...is here!" with a proud look in my direction. Children regard the public presence of their parents as a visible symbol of caring and connectedness that is far more significant than any material support could ever be.

Discussion Questions

1. How would you describe your relationship with your parents when you were growing up? How has it changed as you've become an adult?

2. How would you describe the relationship that you have today with each of your children?

3. What practical steps can you take to strengthen your relationship with your kids? How can your spouse help you make these steps?

Prayer Topic

Spend a few moments praying together. Pray for opportunities to strengthen your relationship with your children. Ask God to help you prioritize your life in a way that both pleases Him and allows you to spend as much time together as a family as possible.

Chapter 7

A Child's Ego Is Like a Family Heirloom

**"Indeed, the very hairs of your head are all numbered.
Don't be afraid; you are worth more than many
sparrows." – Luke 12:7**

Before there was ESPN and other 24-hour sports
channels, ABC's *Wide World of Sports* ruled the airwaves on
Saturday afternoons. Showcasing a wide variety of sports
not normally seen on American television, the show
maintained high ratings throughout the 60s, 70s and 80s. It
is most famous, however, for its iconic opening introduction:

> "Spanning the globe to bring you the constant
> variety of sport...the thrill of victory...and the
> agony of defeat...the human drama of athletic

competition... This is *ABC's Wide World of Sports!*"

The "thrill of victory" and "agony of defeat" soon became catchphrases in the American lexicon, and the image of an unfortunate ski jumper crashing became synonymous with failure.

As a parent, like many parents before me, I too am experiencing the thrill of victory and the agony of defeat as I watch my kids try all sorts of new things, from learning how to ride a bike to tying shoelaces to playing Little League. To be honest, sometimes it is heart-breaking to see them struggle. They take failing very hard (just like their dad). Yet it is amazing what just a little success can do for their confidence.

Once I began staying at home, I realized that my children's self-image was constantly being shaped and reshaped by every victory and every failure that they experienced, no matter how big or how small. Seemingly insignificant struggles like coloring outside the lines brought proclamations about how bad they were at it and how they would never be good artists. Likewise, constructing a garage out of blocks would cause them to pronounce themselves as the world's best builders! Each day was filled with highs and lows, and the emotional roller coaster could be intense and draining.

Dealing with the mental fatigue that comes with leading kids through all of the successes and failures of their day is something that working parents don't really understand. Coming home and hearing how a son or daughter got upset about such minor setbacks can even seem funny, and the response can easily be to simply shake one's head and chuckle a bit. Yet to our kids, these failures are anything but minor!

Failing Vs. Being a Failure

So what is a parent to do? How can we help our kids have healthy and grounded self-images? The task begins with leading them to see that their self-worth is solely achieved through their status as children of God. There is a big difference between failing at something and being a failure, and when we believe in Jesus as our Savior and become part of God's family, being a failure is simply not possible. In Luke 12 Jesus tells His disciples that our worth to God is so great that He knows the number of hairs on our head. The Psalms are filled with passages that extol our value to God.

Psalm 8:3-5 says:

> When I consider your heavens, the work
> of your fingers, the moon and the stars,
> which you have set in place, what is man
> that you are mindful of him? You made
> him a little lower than the heavenly beings
> and crowned him with glory and honor.

We need our children to understand that not only are they God's precious creations, but that God sees them full of glory and honor! This good news gets even better. Consider Psalm 139:17-18:

> How precious to me are your thoughts, O
> God! How vast is the sum of them! Were
> I to count them, they would outnumber
> the grains of sand. When I awake, I am
> still with you.

No matter what we are doing, God always has us on His mind. He is never too busy that he is not concerned about us! One way that we might be able to help our kids understand this better is to talk about fame. Ask them who some famous people are. After they've given their answers, remind them that they are as famous as any of those people. Why? Because the God who created the heavens and the earth knows them by name and thinks about them every second of every day! Can they possibly ever be more famous than that?

Every other way in which we build our self-worth will eventually either let us down or become insignificant. For example, I have a box of cheap plastic trophies in the attic from my baseball playing days. They have never once helped me as an adult. I have never been in a situation where I've been feeling "down" on myself and I've thought, "Well, at least I was the tournament MVP back when I was 12!" When our children's self-worth is based on their athletic ability, or academic achievements, or how good they look, or anything other than the fact that "Jesus loves me, this I know. For the Bible tells me so," then we as parents are focusing them on the wrong things. Our bodies will break down, our memory will erode, and our beauty will fade. Only our relationship with God will last for eternity. This is the truth that we as parents must get through to our kids.

Easier Said Than Done

So the question is, of course, how can we help our kids see their self-worth as coming exclusively from God? The starting place is getting them into His Word. Take them to all of the passages that teach us about how much He loves us. Read them together. Discuss what those verses mean for us and how we should be mindful of them. Write them

and post them in our kids' bedrooms. Memorize them
together. Heed the commands of Deuteronomy 6 and talk
about them "when you sit at home and when you walk along
the road, when you lie down and when you get up."

When our children do fail at something and are upset
about it, we must not ignore their pain or further punish
them. Instead, we need to get them to talk about their
feelings and work with them to decide how they can do
better the next time. For example, if our son comes home
with a poor performance on a spelling test that he had
studied hard for and he is clearly upset, it does him no good
for me to get upset with him and hand down further
punishment. If he tried his best and failed, what good would
sending him to his room or taking away a favorite activity
do? Yes, doing well at school is important, and if he didn't
study or didn't care, my reaction should be different. But if
he did his best and still fell short of the mark, then what he
needs from his dad is not punishment. He needs
encouragement. He needs reminded that Dad still loves him
and so does God. He needs Dad to help him develop a plan
to do better the next time. In the eternal scheme of things,
one poor mark on a test is not significant.

Not surprisingly, the Bible gives clear instruction on
this. Ephesians 6:4 instructs us to not drive our kids to
anger, and Colossians 3:21 reminds us to not exasperate our

children. Think about when you have failed at something. For example, while I will play an occasional round of golf, I am not very good at it. As long as I am playing with others who are there just to have fun, I have a great time. Sometimes, however, there is another player in my group who after every wayward shot or missed putt says something like "Want to know what you did wrong there?" After hearing that about 20 times it takes every fiber in my being not to snap back "NO! It won't make any difference anyway! Worry about your own golf game Mr. PGA Tour!" Is there anything more frustrating than others pointing out your failure to you, especially when you have tried your best? Our kids feel that way too.

While inappropriate punishment can certainly damage our children's sense of self-worth, going to the other extreme and excessively flattering our kids can be just as bad. If we as parents, for example, are constantly singing the praises of our kids' musical ability, then they will soon feel as if that is their identity as persons. As we continue to praise and praise and push and push them, their self-worth becomes tied exclusively to their accomplishments as musicians. Then, when the inevitable time comes that they fail at something as musicians, they are devastated and feel pain at the very core of their being.

Does this mean that we shouldn't praise our kids? Of course not. We should be their biggest supporters! The key is to praise the godly attitudes and attributes that we see our kids using to get their achievements. Praise the effort. Praise the determination and diligence that practice takes in order to be good at something. Praise their ability to work well with others and/or be good teammates. Praise their positive attitude, even when things aren't going their way. The good feelings that achievements bring rarely last long. After all, another game, another test, another recital is just down the road, right? Developing godly character traits, on the other hand, will serve our kids well throughout their lives.

The Agony of Defeat – The Rest of the Story

At the beginning of this chapter I wrote about the poor ski jumper who had the misfortune of having a failure while the TV cameras were rolling (thank goodness all of my failures are not captured on film and played endlessly on TV). What is interesting about the man, a Slovenian named Vinko Bogataj, is that as soon as he got up from his fall, he wanted to get right back on the ski jump and try again! Only the doctors prevented him from doing so.

Many professional athletes have had their lives spiral downward after they've experienced failure in their sport.

The sports world is riddled with stories of men and women who've wasted all the money they earned or have gotten into trouble with the law because their self-worth was derived entirely by their status as athletes, and once that was gone they had nothing to turn to. Certainly Vinko Bogataj could have been one of them, as his failure as an athlete has become synonymous with the "agony of defeat." Yet by all accounts his life barely changed. After retiring as a ski jumper, he went back to his hometown and raised a family with his wife and worked to support them as a factory worker and truck driver. Today he has gained some fame as a painter of landscapes.

So how did Vinko move past his failure? His self-worth was never tied to being an athlete. As he has said during the few interviews he has given since that ill-fated jump, "every time you fall, you have to get back up." When our children's self-worth is grounded in their knowledge that God loves them and cares for them, they too will always be able to get up when they fall.

Discussion Questions

1. How did you handle failure as a child? How do you handle it as an adult?
2. What areas of life do you see your children struggling with right now? What kinds of failures can really hurt their self-confidence?
3. How can you help your kids gain a better understanding of how much God loves and cares for them?

Prayer Topic

Spend a few moments praying together. Pray about the areas of life in which each member of your family is currently struggling. Ask God to help you develop a deeper sense of how much He loves you, and ask Him to help you guide your children to a deeper understanding of that love as well.

Chapter 8

Parenting Is a Tag-Team Sport

**"Listen, my son, to your father's instruction and do not
forsake your mother's teaching." – Proverbs 1:8**

Professional wrestling became hugely popular in the
mid-1980s as the involvement of pop singer Cyndi Lauper
and TV actor Mr. T helped to introduce it to the masses.
My brothers and I were big fans of Hulk Hogan, Hillbilly
Jim, Jimmy "Superfly" Snuka, and all the other heroes of the
World Wrestling Federation (Today I would not let our kids
watch wrestling, as the sexuality and language are far too
extreme for my tastes). One of our favorite types of
matches involved tag-teams. Two pairs of wrestlers would
square off, with two of the combatants in the ring while their
respective partners stood just outside the ropes. Whenever

one of the in-ring wrestlers found himself in trouble, he tagged his partner who then entered the ring to take his place.

While I am no advocate of today's professional wrestling entertainment, tag-team wrestling is a good metaphor for parenting. The stay-at-home parent spends all day "wrestling" with the kids, and is looking for the partner to "tag" in when the working parent arrives home. And "tagging in" needs to involve more than just laying down the law to children who've misbehaved ("just wait till your father gets home").

I've been on both sides of the "ropes." Sometimes when I was home I needed Mary to just take the kids for a little while so I could recuperate, and on more than one occasion I've taken the kids and cleared out of the house so she could have some time to herself. Andy Stanley wrote in the book *"Choosing to Cheat"* that his wife needed him at home during the 4 pm to 6 pm timeframe. That is so true! Trying to cook a nice supper while having kids hanging on your legs, trying to get homework done, or just generally screaming for your attention is nerve-wracking, tiring, and frustrating. Mary and I have reached an understanding that when one of us comes home and the other declares "done," it is time for a tag.

Both Proverbs 1:8 ("Listen, my son, to your father's instruction and do not forsake your mother's teaching") and 6:20 ("My son, keep your father's command and do not forsake your mother's teaching") clearly demonstrate that both Mom and Dad are to be involved in the instruction and training of their children. In many other Near-East cultures of the day, the instruction of children was solely the father's job, but God in His infinite wisdom instructs that both parents are to be involved with the task. Of course, in our western culture the mom usually does not need to be reminded of her role as a parent!

Not surprisingly, virtually all secular and sacred research points to having both parents involved in raising their children as the #1 indicator for a child's success. Yes, there are certainly family situations where having both parents consistently involved in the raising of children is simply not possible. Single parents have a tough job and need all of the encouragement and support that they can get. Just as challenging, however, are those family situations where there appears to be just a "single" parent, even though both Mom and Dad are around!

Tag Team Essential #1 – Love Your Kids

Our kids need to constantly be reminded of two things in order to feel safe and secure at home. The first is that **both Mom and Dad love them**. I cannot stress enough the importance of telling our kids that we love them. I make it a point to tell our kids that I love them at least once a day and strive for more than that.

For many dads, actually saying the words "I love you" is difficult. It doesn't seem like the most "manly" thing to say. We may not have grown up in a home where our dads said it a lot (or ever). Whatever the reason for our hesitation, we need to overcome it. Too often when I speak to groups about parenting, I have someone come to me and say something to the effect of "I never knew if my dad loved me or not." The pain from that neglect often lasts into adulthood.

Tag Team Essential #2 – Love Your Spouse

The second thing that our children need to be reminded of regularly is that **Mom and Dad love each other.** While our kids may recoil if they see Mom and Dad showing each other affection (my kids have been known to run out of the room if Mary and I kiss), secretly they love seeing it, because it reassures them that their family is going to stay together.

Our kids understand all too well what happens when a marriage is in trouble or dissolves because they see the results in their schools, on their sports teams, and in their neighborhoods.

Theodore Hesburgh, the long-time president of the University of Notre Dame, is famously quoted as saying, "The most important thing that a father can do for his children is love their mother." In order to be a great parent, we must first be a great spouse. For some parents (particularly moms) there is a strong temptation to place a higher priority on their kids' lives than their marriage.

Misplaced priorities have harmed many families. Couples who do not make their marriage a top priority in the home risk slowly drifting apart, year by year, until they are essentially roommates with children. Marriages in the "empty nest" years have the second highest divorce rate (trailing only newlyweds), mainly because many couples keep their marriage going solely for the "sake of the children." What these couples fail to realize, however, is the emotional and spiritual damage that growing up in a home with parents who do not love each other can cause.

It is God's plan for couples to prioritize their relationship. Why? Because the kids will eventually leave! Genesis 2:24 states, "For this reason a man will leave his father and mother and be united to his wife, and they will become one flesh." When our kids are gone, it will be just Dad and Mom. We need to have a strong marriage to survive the inevitable sense of loss that becoming empty nesters will bring. If we truly love our kids, we will love our spouse.

Tag Team Essential #3 – We Need a Plan

Very few of us would start a huge undertaking without a plan for success, but many parents seem to raise their kids without any planning at all. What do you want your children to "look like" when they turn 18? What values do you want them to have? What character traits do you want them to develop? What skills and abilities do you want them to possess?

Those are some big questions, and they need answers. Coming up with those answers and then having your children attain the values, abilities, and character traits that you desire for them doesn't happen by accident. Some real thought needs to be put into how you are going to train your children in those areas, and both parents need to know the plan!

Admittedly, suggesting that you have to have a plan for your kids seems a bit cold and distant (and certainly not loving) at first glance. After all, our kids are not machines, and they certainly don't come with a blueprint and/or instruction manual. But when we take a closer look at how we are going to go about raising our kids, I believe that we will quickly see how loving it is to have a plan.

As parents we need to sit down and have some long discussions about what our hopes and dreams are for our kids. Once we have at least a general idea of what those hopes are, we need to consider what kinds of activities, learning experiences, and responsibilities our kids should have in order to realize those hopes. For example, what will teach your kids diligence and personal discipline? What will teach them teamwork and valuing others? Playing sports would help in those areas, and so would learning an instrument or taking part in a drama production. Does your child need to play three different sports, or participate in all three activities to learn those character traits? Perhaps, but then again, perhaps not.

Those questions will need to be answered by both of you, and a wide range of factors (your child's interests, your family's schedule, available opportunities) will help you determine those answers. Very few firm and fast "rules" exist when it comes to parenting, and I often joke that the answer to any parenting question is "it depends." The truth is, however, that "it depends" is often the correct answer. That is why parenting is so fun and challenging – your kids, your family, your situation – they are all unique!

I encourage you to sit down together to talk through your parenting plan – perhaps even write down some things. Set some goals for the coming months and share them with your kids. Explain to them why you are doing what you are doing, and invite their input for the decision-making process.

If you've been the parent who has been "missing in action," don't give up. It's never too late to get involved with your kids. If it's been a while since you've been really engaged, don't worry if that connection you are seeking doesn't happen right away. Give it time, and the relationship will begin to flourish.

If you've been the engaged parent and your partner has been disengaged, invite and encourage your partner to jump in. Sometimes a disengaged parent may see that the engaged parent has things "under control" and be afraid that his or her involvement will only cause problems. Other times the engaged parent may feel that it is just easier to "parent" alone. Whatever the situation may be, recommit to parenting as a team and with a plan.

Discussion Questions

1. How do you demonstrate your love to your kids? How do you know that they are feeling that love?

2. In what areas of your marriage are you strongest? What areas could use some enrichment?

3. Begin to answer some of the questions raised in the "parenting plan" section of the chapter:

   a. What do you want your children to "look like" when they turn 18?

   b. What values do you want them to have?

   c. What character traits do you want them to develop?

   d. What skills and abilities do you want them to possess?

Prayer Topic

Spend a few moments praying together. Pray that you would be able to communicate your love for your children more deeply and more frequently. Pray for your marriage and ask God to continue to bless and protect it. Pray for opportunities to invest in your relationship. Pray for each of your children, and ask God to give you wisdom as you develop your parenting plan.

Chapter 9

Putting It All Together - The Family Pyramid

"But as for me and my household, we will serve the Lord." - Joshua 24:15

Four years and one college degree later, my time as a full-time stay-at-home dad has come to an end. As further proof that God is in control and truly knows what He is doing, I now work for a family ministry. Part of my work involves teaching parenting classes, and my experiences as a stay-at-home dad have certainly enhanced my teaching. While at one time I would look toward the heavens and as why I was staying at home, I now look up and smile as I talk to groups that include many stay-at-home moms. God has uniquely prepared me for my current profession!

The days of waking up in the morning and having the home be my workplace are over, but the lessons that I've learned during those years will stay with me forever. If nothing else, I've found that the key to being a godly parents is to have our priorities in order. If you would have asked me what my top priorities were a few years ago, I would have quickly listed God, family, and work in that order. It sure sounded good, and it was the "Christian" thing to say. The sad truth is, however, that my life certainly didn't reflect those priorities.

Although we often list our priorities from top to bottom in a list, I've found that thinking of them as a pyramid is really helpful. Pyramids such as the Egyptians and Mayans built have lasted for centuries because they were built to last. In order for that to happen, the foundation of the pyramid must be the strongest and largest level, with the next level slightly smaller, and so on and so on. Pyramids that weren't built this way would have been unstable and would have quickly crumbled. No one has ever built a pyramid upside down!

So if we think about what should be the foundation, the strongest part of our personal life and our family's life, and then place each area of our life on top of that in order of priority, we build a strong family that is built to last. So the obvious question is, how should we build our family pyramid?

The Foundation Stone – Our Walk with God

Our first priority in life must be our relationship with God. It is more important than our relationship with our spouse, our kids, or our work. It MUST be our foundation stone!

Too often in life when we find ourselves struggling emotionally, spiritually, or even physically, our priorities have gotten mixed up. It's easy to do! Paul's letter to the Ephesians is a great guide to getting our priorities in order. In chapters 1 – 3 we learn about who we are in Christ. In chapters 4 – 6 we learn how we are supposed to live in Christ. Verses 4:1 – 5:21 discuss our walk with God; 5:22 –32 talk about our walk with our spouse; 6:1-4 tell about our walk with our kids; and 6:5-9 tell about our walk at work. Finally, the book ends with the great passage about putting on the armor of God!

Obviously much more could be said about how to build our relationship to God. Since this is primarily a parenting book, I am going to end this section here and encourage you to seek out other worthwhile resources to help you with pursuing Him.

The Second Level – Our Walk with Our Spouse

Although his prominence in popular culture has subsided over the past few years, many people still recognize the name Ted Turner. Turner became famous in the early 1980s for launching CNN, starting the Goodwill Games, and creating a media empire with several different cable networks. He also bought the Atlanta Braves and helped to turn that franchise into a consistent pennant winner in baseball. In short, Turner was (is) a successful man by almost any measure.

Yet, when asked about his success, Turner once said the following: "After having done CNN and the Superstation, winning the America's Cup in 1977 and the '95 World Series with the Atlanta Braves, I feel I can do just about anything. Except have a successful marriage." It was a shocking admission by a man known for his pride. Ted Turner, largest private landowner in the U.S., wealthy beyond what most can imagine, has had three failed marriages in his life.

Why does a successful marriage seem so elusive? That's a simple question that seems to need a complex answer, but I'm not so sure. When you cut away all of the peripheral issues, the answer to how to have a successful marriage is really a matter of priority. After our relationship with God, our relationship with our spouse is the most important one that we have. Not the one with our boss, not the ones with our friends, not the ones with our parents, not even the ones with our kids.

Even typing that sentence doesn't feel right. It feels as if those other relationships should be very important to us, and they should be. However, our relationship with our spouse must be more important. Our spouse is the one we have pledged to love and to honor. Our spouse is the one who will be with us long after the kids move out, we retire from our job, and Mom and Dad aren't around anymore.

Don't take my word for it. Genesis 2:24-25 states, "For this reason a man shall leave his father and mother and cleave to his wife; and the two shall be one flesh." There is only one person in this world that God designed us to be so close to, that we are to be like "one flesh" – our spouse. In the Pyramid of Priorities, if we put our marriage in any other slot than right behind God, then our marriage is not going to work the way God intends it to work.

Generally speaking, women can struggle with placing their kids before their marriage and men can struggle with placing their jobs before their marriage (although the roles can reverse). Why? I think it's a combination between what our Christian culture expects and what we perceive that God expects. The perception can be that moms are supposed to take care of the kids so they devote all of their time, energy, and devotion to the kids. Dads are expected to be providers so they devote all of their time, energy, and devotion to work. Both have good intentions, but both have their priorities out of whack.

So what can be done? First, make the commitment to your spouse that he or she will always be your top priority after God. Then commit to holding each other accountable and verbalize when you are (or are not) feeling like a top priority. View your time and energy as you do your money – budget it carefully, and pay your most important "bills" first!

The Third Level – Our Walk with Our Kids

We are great at rationalizing our work priority. Have you ever heard (or said) the following?

"I'm putting in a lot of hours right now so that in a few years I won't have to work as hard and can spend more time with the family."

"She's better with the kids when they are little anyway…once they grow up I'll get involved."

"I work hard, and I deserve to be able to play hard as well."

"I use all of my recreation time as networking time, so in a way, I'm being productive even when I'm _____ (hunting, golfing, etc.)."

"I believe in quality time, not quantity time."

Dads, we can justify working (which is a good thing, for the Bible clearly says that we are to work) at the expense of our family all we want, but the fact remains that God intends our priorities to be our relationship to Him, to our wife, to our kids, and then (and only then) to our work. If we place work anywhere else on our pyramid of priorities, we aren't living according to God's plan. According to God, quantity time IS quality time!

The Fourth Level – Our Walk at Work

A popular song in the early 1980s was "Working for the Weekend" by the group Loverboy. The song lyrics (which, admittedly, make very little sense when you read them) contained the catchy chorus "Everybody's working for the weekend. Everybody wants a little romance." Although the song is now 30 years old, that sentiment appears to have remained among society. Everybody, it seems, is still working for the weekend. We work long hours so that we can not only provide for our family, but so that we have enough left over for the "fun" stuff in life. Entertainment, sporting events, big "toys" like jet skis and four-wheelers, eating out – the ways that we can spend our "weekend" dollars is endless. In fact, our recreational opportunities (and the priority that we place on them) have only increased since that song was a hit!

When we look at how God views our work, however, we quickly see that working just so we can have stuff should not be our motivation. God clearly expects us to work. We see counsel on how we should approach our work throughout scripture, so it's obvious that our work is a priority to God. That being said, it is important to remember our Pyramid of Priorities – work comes fourth, after our walk with God, walk with our spouse, and our walk with our kids.

So the big question is, "How does God want us to view our work?" Ephesians 6:5-9 is a good starting point. In verse 7 Paul instructs us to "serve wholeheartedly, as if you were serving the Lord, not men." Talk about a change in perspective! How many Christians view their work as a way to serve the Lord? How can we maintain that outlook on our work, especially when things aren't going well? Here are some ideas to consider.

S ensitive to Needs – Matthew 20 states that whoever wishes to be great must first be a servant. Don't wait to be told to do something at work. If it needs done, do it!

E veryday Diligence – Doing our very best every day is important to God, and it should be important to us as well.

R eaching Others - Wherever we go, whatever we do, our work ought to leave behind an impression that we are seeking to serve God rather than just people. God gives us skills and abilities to build and expand His kingdom. We are expected to use them!

V ictory in Mind - We should work as if Jesus himself was our boss!

E nthusiastically - God wants us to work hard and do our best, even with small responsibilities.

Work can be a source of stress, frustration, and even loneliness. Keeping the proper perspective on both its place in our pyramid and God's view of it in our lives can help make our work more meaningful and fulfilling.

The Challenge

Through the pages of this book I've tried to encourage working parents to consider their role in the family and think about how they can be a more involved parent despite the fact that they must spend many hours a week away from home. I've also tried to encourage stay-at-home parents to be as helpful as possible in integrating the working partner into the family life. Finally, I've encouraged couples to take time to reflect and talk about the struggles that they face in their respective callings and to seek to understand the shoes that their partner walks in.

None of this, of course, is easy. Balancing work and home, raising children with different personalities and abilities, coming together in our marriage when it seems that everything in the world wants to pull us apart, none of our parenting challenges come with simple and easy-to-do answers. That's the "bad news."

Thankfully, the "good news" is that God's grace is always available for us. I do not strive to a "perfect parent," because I know that I will never meet that goal. Instead, I strive to be a "pursuing parent." That is, I strive to pursue God in everything that I do as a parent. I pursue Mary as my partner for life. I pursue a meaningful relationship with our children. I constantly pursue His Word for guidance. I pursue ways to show our kids His love for them. The great part of being a "pursuing parent" – it can be done whether or not we work or we are home with the kids!

I'm still asked the dreaded "So, what do you do?" question these days, and I have to admit that it is nice to be able to talk about my "job." Yet, I've come to realize that no matter what the outcome is of those "title" battles that I have with other men, having the title of "Dad" will always make me the "winner." To become a parent is to receive one of God's greatest blessings while we are on this side of eternity.

Discussion Questions

1. How is your family pyramid looking? Is it built to last, or is it in danger of crumbling?

2. What changes do you need to consider in order to strengthen each level of your pyramid?
    a. Walk with God
    b. Walk with Spouse
    c. Walk with Children
    d. Walk at Work

3. How can you help/encourage your spouse to be a pursuing parent?

Prayer Topic

Spend a few moments praying together. Pray for each level of your pyramid, and ask God to help you keep your priorities in order. Pray for your spouse's pyramid as well and ask for wisdom in helping your spouse. Give thanks for each of your children, and ask God to continue to grant you opportunities to invest in their lives.

ABOUT THE AUTHOR

Born and raised in the southern end of Lancaster County, PA, Scott started attending Memorial United Methodist Church when he was two weeks old and accepted Christ there in 4th grade. After graduating from high school Scott earned a Bachelor's degree in Business Education from Shippensburg University, where he met his wife Mary.

Scott and Mary were married in 1998 and they moved to Smoketown, PA. After teaching at a local high school and working as a Director of Human Resources for a local firm Scott returned to school at Lancaster Bible College and earned his Master of Arts in Ministry degree. Upon completing his internship at House on the Rock Family Ministries, Scott officially joined the team. He currently coordinates all of the ministry activities with House on the Rock's partner churches and speaks frequently throughout the south-central Pennsylvania area. Scott is well-known for the energy and passion that he brings to his speaking!

Mary teaches math at a local college. They are the proud parents of three young children – Greg (age 10), Abby (7) and Trent (3), and are active members of their church.

ABOUT HOUSE ON THE ROCK FAMILY MINISTRIES

House on the Rock Family Ministries exists to help churches build strong marriages and families on Biblical guidelines. We believe that "Families built on the 'Rock' today, will stand the storms of tomorrow."

House on the Rock Family Ministries sees the church as a "family of families." We believe that if we strengthen families we will strengthen churches. We envision helping church leaders develop and implement a vision and strategy for building their families through effective family ministries. We envision offering these ministries Biblically based family life educational events that will help them to strengthen their men, their marriages, their families and ultimately their churches.

We sharpen our focus to envision:

- Godly men becoming the loving servant leaders of their marriages, families and churches.

- Christ centered marriages where couples reflect and demonstrate God's unconditional love to their spheres of influence. Where husbands and wives help each other to become more Christ-like.

- Nurturing parents building Godly families where their children are grounded in the Word of God.

- Church leaders who are committed to supporting and growing their families as a means of growing their churches.

We envision House on the Rock partnering with kindred family oriented ministries. We cannot accomplish our mission alone. If we are to see our vision fulfilled we need to work together with others who have a similar vision. We envision ourselves as the ground troops in the battle for the American family. Our goal is build our ministry so that we can minister effectively within our target area of local churches.

Visit us online at www.hotrfm.org!

HAVE HOUSE ON THE ROCK AT YOUR CHURCH!

We would love to serve as your resource for an one-day event, weekend retreat, or an entire week of meetings. Our workshops are not only informative and interactional, but also lots of fun! Some of our workshops include:

Two Worlds, One Family (based on this book!)

"...and they will become one flesh" For many couples achieving the "oneness" of marriage that is described in the Bible is a difficult challenge because they spend so much of their time in two very different worlds - one at home, the other at work." Two Words One Family" discusses the challenges of being a stay-at-home parent from a guy's perspective and how the working parent and stay-at-home parent can and must support each other's roles and responsibilities.

Who's on Your Pit Crew?

Life is a "rat race" and we can't win alone. We need someone to put air in our tires, gas in our tanks, and clean the debris from our car so that we can run to win! This talk compares the role of a NASCAR pit crew to a small group of men in our lives. We use lots of NASCAR pictures to reinforce the presentation. Men will be strongly encouraged to get connected with other men.

Becoming a Man of Impact

This workshop presents a challenge from the life of Ezra to become a man that impacts his sphere of influence. We challenge men to begin to formulate a purpose statement for their lives. A presentation of the need for "mentoring" is also given and men are challenged to join small groups or to form their own mentoring "circles." The presentation un-packs the 5 letters in IMPACT: **I** - Inspected Life, **M** - Mission, **P** - People to IMPACT, **A** - Action Plan, **C** - Counting the Cost, and **T** - Team to help you.

Reclaiming Intimacy

God created marriage as an unbreakable covenant relationship a man and a woman. This union not only reflects the image of God, it is a mirror into the relationship that exists between the Father, Son and Holy Spirit. Paul wasn't kidding when he said it was a mystery! Reclaiming Intimacy focuses on the three foundational intimacies: emotional, physical, and spiritual. Couples will learn what intimacy is and what it looks like! Time will be given to talk about the condition of these intimacies in your marriage and to plans as to how you can continue to "reclaim intimacy."

Making DEPOSITS into Your Spouse's Emotional Bank

All of us have an emotional bank. We either feel loved and secure, or unloved and insecure. We strengthen our marriages by making regular deposits into our spouses' emotional banks. This event overviews 8 powerful deposits: love languages, encouragement, promises, oneness, spending time, integrity, touch, and spiritual connection that we can make into one another's banks. Couples will enjoy some great knee to knee discussions around these topics.

The 5 Keys to Biblical Parenting

Designed for parents who desire to sharpen their skills, this seminar provides an overview of 5 keys to effective parenting: modeling, controlling, communicating, interacting, and creating character building experiences. Practical examples are plentiful. Included in the workshop is a presentation that surveys the four major parenting styles. Each participant will be "tested" to determine their parenting style. Implications as to how each style impacts children will be presented. A discussion will explain how you can change your parenting style if needed.

His GRAND Scheme

The number of grandparents who are parenting their grandchildren on either a full time or a part time basis is growing daily! Adapted from the book "*Extreme Grandparenting*" by Tim and Darcy Kimmel, this workshop discusses four roles that grandparents can play in the lives of their grandchildren and give some practical strategies on how they can connect to their grandkids on a deeper level. Also great for parents to be a part of, as we discuss how they can help connect their parents to their kids.

This Isn't the Brady Bunch Anymore!

When it comes to stepfamilies, many of the "rules" about parenting and marriage simply don't apply! This workshop is geared towards both couples who are in a stepfamily and those in the church who are not. We discuss some strategies for creating healthy stepfamilies and also point out some of the unique qualities of stepfamilies that individuals and churches (particularly church leaders) need to understand to be able to minister to them effectively.

Tech 101 - Facebook, Filters, and Cell Phones

Keeping up with the ever-changing technology in this world is tough work. This workshop is geared toward helping "unconnected" parents raise "connected" kids. We talk about a Biblical view of technology and talk about the "nuts and bolts" of social media and cell phones, pointing out the dangers that parents should be concerned about.

What's Happening to My Teenager?

This workshop overviews six different areas of adolescent development, including:

Physical Changes	**Social Changes**
Intellectual Changes	**Emotional Changes**
Identity Changes	**Faith and Values Changes**

"What's Happening to My Teenager" will help parents understand the many transitions that are taking place within the lives of their teens.   Practical applications and implications for parenting teens will be discussed!

Families "R" We Weekends

House on the Rock offers churches a unique opportunity. We lead a weekend retreat that ministers to the entire family. Dads, moms, and children interact together around the acrostic FAMILY where each letter represents a dynamic of being a family: Faith building, Affirmation, Merriment, Identity, Love and Yore.

Keeping Your Kids from Canaan: Preparing Them for a Godless World

Learn how to develop and deepen the spiritual life of your children. This presentation highlights the instructions of Moses to the people of God in Deuteronomy 6. Life changing mandates, methods, and motivations are mined from the text. These were given to the Israelites before they entered into the land of the Canaanites ... wealthy, materialistic, idol worshiping -- God hating people ... sound familiar? We as believers can prepare our children to ward off the plague of the Canaanites.

The 4 Laws of Marriage

The **Law of Leave:** "for this reason a man will leave." Our marriages are to be the most important human relationships we have.

The Law of Cleave: "shall cleave" ... the idea of cleaving implies an ongoing pursuit of our partners ... we never stop trying to win their affections.

The Law of Weave: "the two became one flesh" ... one flesh is more than the physical union; we need to be building intimacy in every area of our relationships.

The Law of Believe: "naked and unashamed." Just as the fall separated God and man it also separated man and wife. We will discuss the effects of sin on our marriages and present steps to purity. (This material has been adapted from *"Marriage on the Rock"* by Jimmy and Karen Evans.)

Made in the USA
Charleston, SC
06 February 2012